WORLD WAR II STORIES

WAR ON LAND

D0357842

1485635

WORLD WAR II STORIES
WAR ON LAND

ANTHONY MASTERS

Illustrated by Joyce Macdonald

W
FRANKLIN WATTS
LONDON•SYDNEY

Editors Belinda Hollyer, Louisa Sladen
Editor-in-Chief John C. Miles
Design Billin Design Solutions
Art Director Jonathan Hair

First published in 2004
by Franklin Watts
96 Leonard Street
London
EC2A 4XD

Franklin Watts Australia
45-51 Huntley Street
Alexandria
NSW 2015

ISBN 0 7496 4802 3

A CIP catalogue record for this book is available

from the British Library.

Printed in Great Britain

CONTENTS

PROLOGUE   6

DUNKIRK   10

TOP SECRET MISSION   34

OPERATION BARBAROSSA   60

D-DAY   76

PROLOGUE

The Second World War

After the First World War ended in 1918, the countries that had fought in the war worked out a peace settlement. They met in 1919, in a French palace called Versailles, so the settlement was called the Treaty of Versailles.

Because Germany had been defeated, it had to agree to harsh terms. All Germany's overseas empire and some of its European lands (such the Rhineland) were taken by the countries that had won. Germany also had to pay enormous fines every year. The country and its people became very poor.

By the early 1930s, Germany was the poorest nation in Europe. The German people resented that. They wanted big changes that would improve their economy, and restore their self-esteem. They needed a strong and popular leader. Adolf Hitler offered to be that leader, and to make those economic changes – fast. He swept to power in 1933, and soon improved the German economy.

Britain and France were busy with their own economic problems. Their leaders missed the warning signs that Hitler and his National Socialist (Nazi) Party were dangerous and power-hungry. They even praised Hitler's achievements. But his government clamped down hard on the German press and parliament. Hitler became a dictator. It was almost impossible to oppose Nazi policies inside the country.

Hitler invaded the Rhineland in 1936, and Austria in 1938. Many people in Europe still did not see the danger. They thought the Germans were just reclaiming land that had been theirs before, or where mostly German people lived. In 1938, European leaders signed an agreement allowing Hitler to claim the Sudetenland (a border region of Czechoslovakia where mainly Germans lived), in order to maintain peace.

But when Hitler attacked Poland on 1 September 1939, the British and French governments could delay no longer. They had offered to protect Poland against invasion, and they now agreed that German expansion had to be stopped. Neither Britain nor France were prepared or equipped to fight, but two days later they declared war on Germany.

A few countries remained neutral, but the six-year conflict involved almost the whole of the rest of the world, and caused the deaths of millions of people.

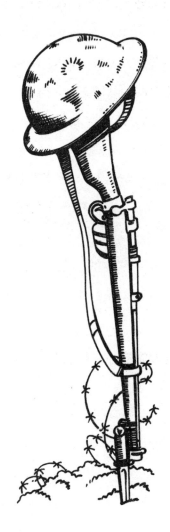

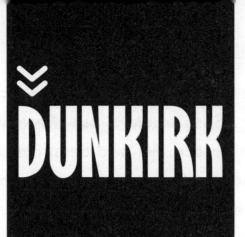

DUNKIRK

I waited on the beach with thousands of other British soldiers, but there was no sign of rescue. We had been continually bombed by German planes. Dawn slowly lightened the night sky while black smoke rose from blazing oil tanks. Nothing moved on the sea.

In the harbour there were only shipwrecks, and the quayside itself was shattered by German bombs. The town

*and docks of Dunkirk were burning
fiercely.*

Still we waited. Still no sign of rescue.

*We knew that the German pilots were
playing cat-and-mouse with us. Soon the
bombing would start again.*

Germany's invasion of Poland in September
1939 was successful. The British and French
thought France would be the next target.
On 11 October the British Expeditionary
Force landed in France to help defend the
country. But the German attack in the west
didn't come until May 1940. First, Germany
invaded Holland, Belgium and Luxembourg.
Those neutral countries had been anxiously
watching Germany's expansion, but they
had not declared war.

Britain and France soon saw how well-
equipped and trained the Germans were.

Their military plans ran well,
and the speed of their tank
attacks took everyone by surprise.
The Germans were able to drive back the
French army, and cut them off from the
British Expeditionary Force. Then the
British troops began to retreat towards
the French coast.

By the end of May 1940, Allied troops
were trapped at Dunkirk on the coast of
northern France, close to the Belgian border.
Hitler's tanks were only a ten-day drive away
from them.

The British Commander-in-Chief, Lord Gort, sent an urgent message to the War Cabinet (the government's war advisers). He said that an escape must be made by sea. If this didn't happen immediately, the whole of the British Expeditionary Force could be killed or captured.

Already Dunkirk was under heavy bombardment from the Luftwaffe (the German air force). While bombs continued to rain down, some of the Allied soldiers tried to shelter in cellars in the town. Others threw away their weapons and set up camp on the beaches, hoping for rescue. They all feared that the German soldiers would soon arrive and take them prisoner, or kill them.

The propaganda leaflets dropped by German planes sounded reassuring. "Put down your arms!" Surely that was an

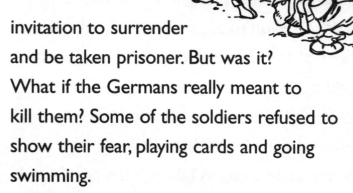

invitation to surrender
and be taken prisoner. But was it?
What if the Germans really meant to
kill them? Some of the soldiers refused to
show their fear, playing cards and going
swimming.

The people who lived in Dunkirk tried
to escape the shattered town, or took
shelter with the trapped Allied soldiers.
There was an atmosphere of rising fear
and panic. Some people got drunk; others
prayed and sang hymns. Perhaps the
strangest sight were the groups who had
settled in deserted cafés, sipping drinks and
looking almost like tourists.

German bombs continued to fall.

The British Second Anti-Aircraft Brigade, with its searchlights and both heavy and light guns, was in charge of protecting Dunkirk. But the Brigade was based several kilometres up the coast at La Panne. The Brigade's Liaison Officer, Captain Sir Anthony Palmer, kept his guns firing at German aircraft for as long as possible.

That gave some cover to the wounded soldiers trying to join the others waiting on the beach. An increasingly desperate crowd scanned the horizon. The soldiers could imagine the white cliffs and shingle beaches of England just across the English Channel, where their families were waiting for them. But the grey waters of the Channel seemed an impossible barrier.

The German bombing continued, and the Allies simply did not have the fire-power to match it. The only chance of escape lay with the sea. Drunk or sober, most men hoped that Britain's Royal Navy would miraculously appear and rescue them. But still they saw no ships.

Then, hours later, a large British destroyer sailed slowly into view. The ship was followed by three barges and fourteen fishing boats, each of them towing a couple of small craft. A sudden surge of hope gripped the men on the beaches. But, by this time, more than 300,000 soldiers were waiting to be rescued.

Further up the coast, three British sloops – small, armed war vessels – were also lying offshore. But the sloops had no rowing boats which could go into the shallow water and fetch the men aboard.

The crisis was getting worse.

The German tanks continued to advance and the bombs continued to fall. There was

an atmosphere of doom. Many soldiers
began to doubt that rescue would come
at all. Someone had to do something fast.

A Royal Marines officer called J. L. Moulton was also scanning the horizon for ships. Finally, he saw a motor-launch approaching the beach. Moulton stumbled over the pebbles and grabbed the prow of the launch to prevent it getting swamped by the surf. But the boat's skipper misunderstood, and thought that Moulton was attempting a hijack. He fired a warning shot over Moulton's head.

Despite the thundering noise of the surf, Moulton managed to explain the desperate situation to the skipper. Once he understood, the captain ferried Moulton out to one of the sloops. Moulton then persuaded yet another captain to take him back across the Channel to England.

Without any authorisation, Moulton went straight to the office of Vice-Admiral Bertram Ramsey, who was in charge of the rescue operation. Moulton hoped Ramsey could improve things. But Ramsey already knew there were thousands of men on the beaches at Dunkirk, and not nearly enough boats to rescue them.

Ramsey had contacted a great many ferries and pleasure-steamers, and he hoped to despatch at least two of them to Dunkirk every three and a half hours – although he knew this would not be anything like enough to ferry *all* the men.

Worse still, the first few rescue boats had already come under

attack from German planes firing machine guns and cannon shells at them.

Soon Ramsey's staff were calling up every single vessel they could contact on the south and east coast of England. These ranged from trawlers and fishing boats to cabin cruisers and yachts.

It was a frustratingly slow process. But the flotilla of boats eventually began to pick up some of the soldiers, who waded out into the sea to board them.

Those on the beaches were trying to make an orderly escape in the face of a barrage of German bullets, shells and bombs. But the onslaught was taking its toll,

and many were killed or injured.

An Isle of Man steamer limped back to Dover, badly damaged, with some survivors. But 23 men had been killed and 60 injured. Instead of taking the usual three hours to cross the Channel, it had taken 11 hours.

As two small coasters neared the French beaches a shell hit one of them, piercing right through her hull, coming out again on the other side. Another shell entered the

engine room and knocked out her pumps. She began to list badly and then to sink. The other coaster picked up her crew from the water and went full steam towards England until she was out of range of the attack.

Ramsey decided that a change of route for the rescue would help. So far the most direct route from Dover to Dunkirk had been a disaster because of the German bombing. Ramsey had to find another route, and quickly.

In fact there were two alternatives. Route X was to the north-east of Dunkirk, so it would avoid the German

bombardment. But the sea was full of mines – floating bombs that could blow up the ships. Route Y was even further away to the north-east, almost as far as the Belgian port of Ostend.

It had been swept free of mines and it was out of range of the German guns. Route Y was the one Ramsey decided on. This turned out to be a good decision.

The *Royal Daffodil*, sailing on Route Y, managed to pick up 900 men. But while the *Daffodil* was within the shattered harbour of Dunkirk, the other ships with her had to anchor outside. If any of them was sunk and blocked the harbour mouth, it would be impossible to rescue any more soldiers.

That evening, another four vessels and a couple of hospital ships, specially equipped to treat the wounded, sailed across on Route Y. They picked up hundreds more men, although they were under heavy fire from the Luftwaffe. Dunkirk harbour was now in ruins, so the beaches became the only escape route.

The British government was desperate. It broadcast a radio appeal for anyone in England who had a sailing boat to help rescue the British Army.

The response was amazing. So was the courage of both amateur and professional sailors who volunteered to sail their boats to France and pick up British soldiers. They returned again and again, despite heavy air attacks from the Luftwaffe. To Hitler's fury, the fleet of small boats successfully rescued over 300,000 soldiers from the beaches. There were many stories of bravery in those hours. Able Seaman Samuel Palmer's story is one of them.

Palmer had taken command of a motor yacht named *Naiad Errant*. About three miles away from Dunkirk he saw a French destroyer making her way into port. When he next glanced that way again, "there was nothing there," he later explained. "She must have taken a direct hit from a bomb and sunk within a few minutes."

Palmer picked up about twenty of the survivors from the destroyer and put them on board a French tug. Then he sailed on towards Dunkirk. Finally, he reached the beaches, where thousands of Allied soldiers were gathered. He recalled: "Three of our little convoy of eight had arrived. The first immediately filled with men and carried on

back to England. The second went aground."

Palmer's first job was to transport some of the soldiers from the beach to a bigger ship. He made a number of trips. Then he tried to help the boat that had run

aground, "but the young seaman with me got the tow rope around my propellers, the result being that I had to give the job up and that my own ship ran aground".

Refusing to admit defeat, Palmer then jumped over the side into the sea. He helped carry wounded soldiers to a larger ship's lifeboat. Then the lifeboat ferried the soldiers on to a bigger ship and safety.

The last boat left the Dunkirk beaches on 4 June 1940. Before leaving, the British Expeditionary Force sabotaged 64,000 of their own vehicles. They disabled hundreds of tanks and over 2,000 guns so that these weapons wouldn't be captured and used by the Germans. But the loss of all those weapons created a huge problem for the British Army. Factories in the UK were put on overtime, working to produce more.

On the afternoon of 29 May 1940, British Prime Minister Winston Churchill had called together the 24 government ministers who were not in the War Cabinet itself. He told them: "Of course, whatever happens at Dunkirk, we shall fight on."

When Dunkirk was over, Churchill made one of his most famous radio broadcasts.

"We shall fight on the beaches,
we shall fight on the landing grounds,
we shall fight in the fields
     and in the streets,
we shall fight in the hills;
we shall never surrender."

TOP SECRET MISSION

On the evening of 6 July 1944, a group of prisoners at the Natzweiler concentration camp watched Diana Rowden and three other women being marched by Nazi SS officers into the Zellenbau – a block of cells that was a prison within a prison.

None of the prisoners ever saw the four women again.

A month after the mass evacuation of British soldiers from the Dunkirk beaches – on 22 June 1940 – France surrendered to

Germany. The war in Europe continued, but now it had to be fought in a different way.

In the countries occupied by Germany, small groups of local people, known as Resistance fighters, secretly fought the Nazis. They damaged railway lines, bridges and other communications. They destroyed factories that manufactured weapons. They helped Allied airmen whose planes had been shot down to escape back to England.

In Britain, Winston Churchill decided to help the Resistance by setting up a Special Operations Executive, or SOE. The SOE would defend Britain if the country was invaded, and support local opposition to the Germans in occupied Europe.

The SOE was top secret. It was known only to the agents who belonged to it, to a few members of the air force, and to the existing intelligence service, MI6. (In fact, MI6 was unwilling to accept the SOE, and thought they were dangerous amateurs. So the two organisations often ended up in competition, each with their own secret agents in the same area.)

Every German-occupied country had its own SOE section in London. The sections recruited agents who were fluent in their language and were good at playing a part. These agents came from many different backgrounds and were often unusual people, with unusual skills.

One of the most intelligent agents in the French section of the SOE was Diana Rowden. Rowden was British but she had been brought up in France, and longed to help liberate her adopted country. But there didn't seem to be any way she could do that, so she joined the Women's Auxiliary Air Force (WAAF). A few days later, however, Rowden was offered just the kind of work she was looking for, from the SOE staff. She was excited and relieved. At last she could start helping to liberate France.

During training, Diana Rowden was described by one of her instructors as "not very agile, but with plenty of courage." She did some "excellent stalks" and was "a very good shot, not at all gun-shy, and her grenade throwing was also good." The final report described Diana Rowden as "a strange mixture, intelligent, but slow in learning new subjects." She had trouble with "technical details", and her signalling was described as "a grief to herself and others, not worthwhile persevering with." The examiner concluded that she hated being beaten by any subject so she "must have got through a lot of hate down here." Nevertheless, he felt she "could be useful".

In spite of this somewhat lukewarm praise, at midnight on 16 June 1943, Rowden was parachuted into France with two other female SOE agents. She landed in a moonlit meadow a few miles north-east of Angers in the Loire valley.

The women had to deliver secret information for the organisers of

various secret communications channels around occupied France. Rowden was sent to the Jura mountains, south-east of Dijon, to work with a local SOE organiser, John Starr, whose code name was "Bob". To equip her for this dangerous job, she was given a coded question to ask when she met up with someone who might – or might not – be a Resistance colleague:

"Is the fishing good around here?" Rowden was instructed to ask.

The correct answer was: "Yes. I caught ten fish last time I went." The number of fish caught had to be the same as the day of the month when she and the contact met. If the answer was incorrect, then she didn't pass on any information.

Diana Rowden was also given a personal coded identity so she could communicate directly with London in an emergency.

Rowden had an unusual personality which made her ideal for such dangerous work. A schoolfriend, Elizabeth Nicholas, remembered her as "one of the most reticent people I have ever met." Nicholas also recalled how Rowden reacted to school. "She was of it, but never part of it. She was too mature for us. We were still schoolgirls in grubby white blouses concerned with games and feuds and ha-ha jokes. She was already adult and withdrawn from our diversions; none of us, I think, ever knew her."

Rowden was given an address in Lisbon, Portugal, as a contact in case her false identity was discovered. (Portugal was a neutral country, like Switzerland.) She might have to escape from France to Portugal, and then to Britain. Her papers were under the name of Juliette Therese Rondeau, but among her fellow agents she

was known as "Paulette". Her code name for use in messages to London was "Chaplain". There was a lot to remember.

Diana Rowden cycled over the mountain roads delivering messages. Sometimes she took messages to Marseilles, Lyon and Paris, and then she used public transport which was even more dangerous.

Rowden had secret meetings with local members of the Resistance. At night, she helped set up flares and used electric torches to guide planes that were making parachute drops of arms and ammunition. On one particular occasion these weapons, as well as explosives, were to be used in an attempt to destroy the Peugeot factory in Montbeliard. The factory had been taken over by the Germans to manufacture engine parts for the Luftwaffe, and tank turrets for the Wehrmacht (the German army).

The Peugeot buildings were located in a heavily populated part of Montbeliard. They had already been the target of British air attacks. But bombing a specific building was very difficult, and sometimes the bombs missed their targets completely, hitting the houses of ordinary French people and causing many deaths. So an attack from the ground seemed a better way to destroy the factory.

Communications were very bad. The SOE had no idea whether the Royal Air Force would try to bomb the factory again, so they had to assume it could happen at any time. But a member of the Peugeot family agreed to brief the Resistance on the layout of the factory. The family hoped that would speed up plans for a ground attack, and so avoid another disastrous air raid.

Eventually the factory was successfully

destroyed, but, soon after, Rowden's local boss, John Starr, was betrayed by a double agent somewhere in the section.

Because of John Starr's arrest, the SOE agents' cover might be blown at any moment. So Rowden hid in a small bistro and shop at Epy, a remote village up in the Jura hills.

She helped in the shop, and the owner had this to say of her. "I knew that she was not accustomed to do such things ... she was a woman of refinement and education, but she was without vanity. She said the work would help her not to be bored."

A local family who owned a saw-mill also helped the Resistance. One branch of the family, the Janier-Dubrys, allowed Diana Rowden and another agent, John Young, to hide in their house. Young was a wireless operator who sent and received secret messages. He could not pass as French, and yet it was essential that he kept on the move with his radio equipment, because the Germans were skilled at tracking down the signals.

Rowden feared that her description had been circulated, so she made some changes to her appearance. She dyed her hair, changed its style, borrowed some new clothes and threw away her old outfits. She also dropped her "Paulette" alias, taking on

the new identity of "Marcelle".

To back this up, the Janier-Dubry family claimed "their cousin Marcelle had come to the country to recover from a serious illness."

The lie was hardly necessary, because most people in the French countryside were helping the Resistance. But there was always a danger of enemy agents, as well as French people who were bribed by the Germans to check out local activities.

As a precaution, Rowden stayed inside, and left the house only to walk through local woods. The woods were thick with trees, and Rowden and Young decided that they could hide there if the Germans did track them down.

Again, Rowden helped in the household, involving herself in domestic tasks and playing with the children, who loved her.

But the safe haven did not last. In November 1942, John Young received a radio message from London. A new agent was arriving, code-named "Benoit". Both Rowden and Young were eager to meet him. They knew Benoit would bring news from London about the war's progress. Hidden away in rural France, and despite the coded radio messages, they had no real idea of what was happening in Britain – or in any of the other countries involved in the war.

At 7.30 on the morning of 18 November, Rowden watched the village street from behind a curtain. A man walked down the road towards the house, wearing a fur-trimmed flying jacket. Was it Benoit?

After identifying himself, the man produced instructions for Rowden and Young, which had been hidden in a matchbox. In order to back up his identity, he also gave Young a letter from his wife, who had very distinctive handwriting.

Benoit said he had to return to a nearby town, Lons-le-Saunier, to pick up a suitcase he had left there. Monsieur Janier-Dubry offered to drive Benoit into town, and Rowden decided to accompany them. Her daily routine of domestic chores and walking in the woods had become boring, and she longed for a change of scene.

In Lons they met a Resistance worker from St Amour called Henri Clerc. All four had a drink at the Café Strasbourg, which was often used as a safe place for agents passing on secret information.

Rowden, Janier-Dubry and Benoit returned to the house, where dinner was being prepared. Suddenly the front door was pushed open and the German military police burst in, armed with machine guns.

Rowden, Young and Benoit were handcuffed and taken away for questioning.

In fact, Benoit was a German agent. Later, he returned to the house with the military police and searched every room, looking for Young's radio equipment, and the crystals that operated it.

The Germans searched the house thoroughly, but found nothing. They did arrest one member of the family who was then sent to Ravensbruck, a German concentration camp where thousands of people died. Amazingly, he survived, and returned after the war. But in the end, the rest of the Janier-Dubry family was let off lightly. They could all have been shot for sheltering two British spies. As punishment, however, the family's jewellery, and any other valuable property they had, was confiscated by the Germans.

While the Germans were searching the house, another member of the Janier-Dubry family – Madame Juif – had found the crystals from Young's radio set in the pocket of his raincoat, hanging behind the front door. Madame Juif slipped the crystals under the mattress in her baby's cot. The Germans never found them.

The next day Rowden was taken to Paris. She was imprisoned at the Gestapo (Nazi secret police) headquarters in the Avenue Foch for two weeks. Then she was transferred to the grim and fortress-like Fresnes prison, a few kilometres outside Paris. Rowden was locked up alone in a cell, and probably tortured by the Gestapo. It was a terrible time for her.

Later, Rowden and three other women agents were transferred to Natzweiler, a concentration camp in Germany.

Emil Bruttel, a medical orderly at Natzweiler, later talked about the four women who were arrested in Paris. He knew they were to be executed after "special treatment".

"We went into a little room," Bruttel said, "where there were several beds. It was here that we learnt from the explanations given by the doctors the details of the plan."

Many of the German doctors who worked at the prison camps had been forced to work there and to administer death instead of trying to cure or to heal.

The doctors told the women that they were being vaccinated against typhus. But that was a lie: they were being killed.

Rowden was injected in her arm with 10 cc of liquid phenol - a deadly poison. One doctor gave the injection. Another doctor checked her pulse and then said, "Death has taken place."

The bodies of Diana Rowden and her companions were then burned in the crematorium ovens in the camp.

In May 1948 *The Times* newspaper in
London ran these headlines:

**TABLET
UNVEILED**

**BRAVE WOMEN
HONOURED**

**SECRET AGENTS
WHO GAVE
THEIR LIVES**

The newspaper article then went on:

"Some of the bravest figures of the war are commemorated among the names of fifty-two women to whose memory a modest tablet was unveiled yesterday ... Of these women and girls, thirteen met death in German prison camps, after having been parachuted into enemy-occupied territory as secret agents to serve the Allies by aiding the Resistance movements ... There is no formula by which to calculate how much cold courage was embodied in these thirteen women, or what they endured in dying for their countries."

As her school friend Elizabeth Nicholas remembered, Diana Rowden had always longed for the life she had led in France, "... for the yachts and the sea and the warm sun of the Mediterranean ..."

The freedom to live that life was the very freedom that she died defending.

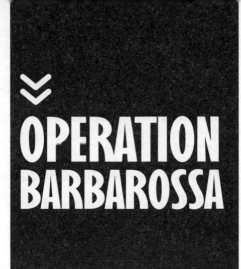

OPERATION
BARBAROSSA

Even in September before the advent of winter there was incessant rain and a cold north-easterly wind, so that every night there was the scramble for shelter, squalid and dung-ridden as it was ... All ranks were filthy and bearded, with dirty, rotting and lice-ridden underwear: disease was shortly to follow.

From the diary of a young German soldier in the Russian countryside, September 1941

When Hitler invaded Austria in 1938, the communist leaders in the USSR (the Soviet Union) knew his expansion would continue.

So Stalin, the Soviet leader, offered to help the British and

French armies defend Czechoslovakia if that country came under German attack. Stalin wanted to stop Hitler's eastern advance.

But the British rejected the Russian offer. So when the German army marched into Prague in March 1939, Stalin had to find another way to protect the Soviet Union.

Hitler hated and feared communism, but in August 1939 he signed a non-aggression pact with Stalin. That meant Stalin could delay going to war with Hitler, and also acquire more territory for the Soviet Union. When Germany invaded Poland from the west, the Soviets attacked from the east. They divided the country between them.

Encouraged by this success, Stalin next attacked Finland. The Finns resisted fiercely, and finally surrendered in March 1940. But Hitler watched the Soviet army's difficulties and the Finns' courageous struggle. He thought it meant that the Soviet Red Army wasn't strong or well-organised. He decided that the non-aggression pact had run out.

The occupation of France gave Hitler a good launching pad for the invasion of Britain. But instead, he decided to invade the Soviet Union. This plan – code-named Operation Barbarossa – began in June 1941. Greece had finally surrendered to the Germans, and the weather had improved, so the conditions were judged right. But it was not as easy as Hitler confidently expected.

A German general recalled how tough the going was for the German army once the invasion had taken place. Russia, the main country in the Soviet Union, had few modern roads. Its terrain was very difficult and its climate was extreme. But most of all, "the Russian civilian was tough and the Russian soldier still tougher," said the general. The soldiers "seemed to have an unlimited capacity for obedience and endurance."

Stalin, too, had misjudged the situation. He had dismissed international warnings about the invasion. His army commanders hadn't set up defences along the German-Russian border, because Stalin thought such defences would provoke Hitler into breaking their pact.

Stalin knew that Hitler was capable of enormous risks. But he was certain that Hitler wouldn't take the greatest risk of all – invading the USSR – unless the USSR attacked Germany. He was convinced that if he remained friendly, so would Hitler. Stalin was still sending trainloads of oil, grain and other supplies to Hitler's Germany as German troops were gathering at the Soviet border.

Operation Barbarossa began on 22 June 1941. Using 165 divisions and 2,500,000 men, the Germans planned a three-pronged attack. At first this was highly successful.

One young German soldier remembered what happened. "The Panzer divisions (tank forces) worked their way swiftly through the Russian countryside, heading for Moscow, Leningrad and Kiev. ... We marched behind them as fast as we possibly could. We knew we had to not only keep up the advance, but mop up resistance as we went."

Stalin didn't believe reports of the German advances. He refused to let the Russian army retreat. Thousands of Russian soldiers were taken prisoner, and many Russian air force planes were shot down by the Luftwaffe as well.

"We were sure we were going to be inside Moscow in six weeks," said the German soldier. But the Soviets fought back fiercely. The same German soldier remembered the Russian soldier as "a formidable enemy, largely because, unlike us, he was prepared to fight to the death."

The Soviet troops had good reason to fight hard. Cowards risked execution by their fellow soldiers. And if they were taken prisoner, the Soviet soldiers knew they would receive terrible treatment. In fact, 3,300,000 Soviet prisoners-of-war died in German prison camps.

Then, at the end of July 1941, Hitler ordered his Panzers not to take the major Russian cities until the infantry (foot soldiers) caught up with them.

Many senior German commanders

realised that was a mistake. The deadly Russian winter, when it arrived, would be the most powerful enemy of all. The German army could only win if they took the big cities before winter. But the delay that Hitler ordered made that extremely unlikely. Some officers resigned in protest.

By September 1941 the German army had captured the Russian cities of Riga, Smolensk, Kiev and Minsk, and 665,000 Russian soldiers had been captured. Stalin hit back with a "scorched earth" policy. This meant his army set Russian villages on fire as they retreated, slowing the Germans and destroying vital supplies.

The German army's delay in seizing Russian cities gave Leningrad and Moscow time to prepare for the onslaught. Their inhabitants built defences, including anti-tank ditches and fortress-like earthworks.

By the time the cold, wet autumn weather arrived, the German soldiers were exhausted. The roads had become rivers of mud, and German tanks got bogged down.

In October, the frost had set in as well. This caused the German soldiers great hardship, but at least the ground was firm again. The German tanks could get on the move once more.

The German army almost succeeded in invading Moscow. They got as far as one of the suburbs of the Russian city. But in the process, more than 200,000 men died.

Five months of hard fighting had taken their toll on the German army. Soon it was the middle of winter and the soldiers faced extreme cold. They were unable to advance any further.

"Moscow had been saved," remembered a German soldier. But their enemy "was not the Russians. It was frostbite."

Worse still, the exhausted German army didn't have the right clothes for winter. Their coats couldn't keep out the bitter wind and the sub-zero temperatures.

The same German soldier remembered how conditions had been for them. "There could be no question of retreat. We were practically frozen to the spot. But another

reason for not retreating was that Hitler had ordered us not to do anything of the kind. We had to stay. We had to fight. We had to freeze."

The German army fought in Russia for more than two more years. It was a terrible time for both them and the Russian people. But the Soviet leaders refused to give in.

Eventually, Soviet determination triumphed. Following the battles of Stalingrad and Kursk, between March and April 1944 the Red Army reclaimed

265 kilometres of territory. Soon they had freed their major cities. Thousands of German soldiers were taken prisoner, because Hitler still refused to allow any of his troops to retreat.

By early 1944 the Red Army had pushed the Germans back to the Polish border. From the German army's point of view, Operation Barbarossa was a disaster. But it helped the Allies. The German campaign forced the Soviet Union to join the Allies, and fight against the Nazis.

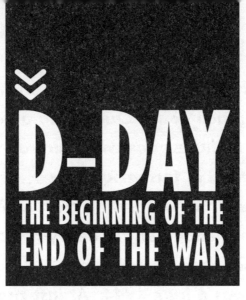

D-DAY

THE BEGINNING OF THE
END OF THE WAR

Ships of every type were at anchor off the French coast. Out to sea a battleship fired its huge guns while aircraft roared overhead in formation.

Hundreds of landing craft laden with troops headed under heavy fire towards the beaches of Normandy.

It was 6 June 1944. At last the Allies had begun the campaign to drive Nazi forces out of the European countries they had occupied since 1940.

In order to surprise Nazi commanders, the planners of Operation Overlord – or "D-Day", as it became known – had set up an elaborate deception. The Allies wanted Hitler to believe that Calais, on the French coast, was to be the target of the invasion. In fact, an area about 240 kilometres to the south-west was chosen. The landings were to be made on the relatively unfortified beaches of Normandy. They were code-named Utah, Omaha, Gold, Juno and Sword.

This part of coastal France was closest to the industrial centres of Germany. Also, the attack could easily be supported by fighter aircraft based in England, just thirty kilometres away across the English Channel.

The Allies made complicated attempts to fool the Germans. They assembled a vast array of rubber tanks and plywood ships at ports in southern England. The lines of tents in the "army encampments" nearby were actually empty, although special stoves blew smoke through their chimneys. Planes and oil depots were also fake.

In fact, the Germans never knew where the Allied forces would invade. General Glumentritt, Chief of Staff to the German Commander-in-Chief, remembered later

that from the intelligence point of view "very little reliable news came out of England." He added: "There were a small number of German agents in England who reported by wireless transmitter sets what they observed. But … nothing we learnt

gave us a definite clue where the invasion was actually coming."

At dawn on 6 June 1944, 8,000 British and American troops parachuted into Normandy. There they captured essential bridges, and disrupted as many German lines of communications as they could. Eventually, because Hitler had been out-witted, over 150,000 Allied troops landed successfully on the Normandy beaches.

By 10.15 a.m. the German commander Field-Marshal Rommel, who was still in Germany, learned of the landings. He flew back to France with Hitler's orders to drive the invaders back into the sea by midnight.

But the Allies were well established. Hitler had waited too long, and Operation Overlord had gained an Allied foothold in Normandy.

Allied dead and wounded figures were lower than expected, except at Omaha Beach where the Americans suffered heavy casualties. William Ryan of the US 16th Infantry Regiment was among the first American soldiers to land on Omaha Beach. He was eighteen, and this was the first time he had been in action.

Ryan had boarded his transport ship at Weymouth on 2 June 1944, but bad weather delayed the sailing. Eventually they left on 6 June, and the crossing was so rough that "most of the men were so seasick they didn't care whether they lived or died. They were too sick to be scared."

Ryan's company had been ordered to Omaha Beach in six landing craft. They were immediately swamped by heavy seas.

The sailor steering Ryan's landing craft lost his bearings; they were soon off course. Eventually he recovered direction, only to find other craft blocking the way. So they had to wait offshore, where they were sitting ducks for German planes.

Soon German shore-based guns had Ryan's boat in range and Ryan was "blown over the side and knocked unconscious." He was later told that "two of the men in the boat with me dragged me through the water and propped me up. Otherwise I would have drowned." Ryan also said that, "… at first there were four or five wounded with me. Then there were hundreds. I laid on the beach in the same position from about 8 a.m. until 10 p.m."

Ryan had shell fragments in his shoulder, head and leg, and throughout that long day he slid in and out of consciousness. But he was lucky to be alive. American troops

were under constant fire from the German guns. Eventually a US Navy destroyer came as close to the beach as it could, and shelled the German positions. Other American ships joined in later.

William Ryan said it was the skipper of that American destroyer who helped win

the battle of Omaha Beach. He recalled: "I heard afterwards that the commander of the ship was ordered to go back to a safe position, but didn't budge. Apparently he wasn't leaving while our soldiers were pinned down on the beach. He could have been in serious trouble for disobeying orders. But he should have got a medal."

Omaha Beach was a savage battle for the inexperienced American soldiers taking part. The first wave of troops was mostly killed, cut down as they came ashore. Then the second wave of troops had to advance over the bodies of the dead. Survival was their main instinct.

Reverend R. Myles Hickey, a Canadian Roman Catholic chaplain (military priest) was with the British and Canadian assault force that stormed Juno Beach. The Allied soldiers trying to make a landing there were sprayed with German machine-gun fire and shells. The noise was deafening. Allied soldiers couldn't even hear the sound of their own tanks thundering across the sand, above the noise of the bombardment. Hickey recalled the fearful suddenness with which some of his fellow soldiers met their deaths: "When a shell came screaming over, you … waited for the blast and the shower of stones and debris that followed; then, when it cleared a little, right next to you, someone you had been talking to half an hour before lay dead."

He remembered that he could tell what religion the soldiers belonged to by the little discs that hung around their necks. But even if the soldier that Hickey was looking after was not a Roman Catholic, he would tell the man he was dying and to be sorry for his sins. "Often I was rewarded by

the dying man opening his eyes and nodding
to me knowingly."

In his account of the assault on Juno
Beach, Hickey particularly praised the
courage of the first-aid men and the
stretcher bearers who carried the wounded
men to safety; but Hickey was no less brave
in his efforts to comfort the dying.

Although the number of soldiers killed at Juno sounds high – 2,500 – it was not very large for an operation on this scale. The German army was simply not in place in sufficient numbers to combat the invasion.

The Allies now had the difficult job of capturing German-held Normandy towns.

As the Allies secured the beach-head (the part of the shoreline they had captured from the enemy) French citizens rushed to offer them food and drink, and help the wounded. By the end of the day the five beach-heads were secure and the German forces were disorganised and confused.

At the start of the day, Hitler had been convinced that the Allied landings were a false alarm. He had refused to release two Panzer divisions from eastern France to go to Normandy. As the invasion progressed, of course, he deeply regretted his decision.

When American troops reached the suburbs of the town of Cherbourg, the German commander, General Karl Wilhelm von Schlieben, was desperate to surrender. He appealed to Field-Marshal Rommel: "Amongst the troops defending the town there are two thousand wounded who cannot be treated. Is the sacrifice of the others still necessary?"

But Rommel's reply was terse. "In accordance with the Führer's ("Führer" is the German word for "leader") orders, you are to hold out to the last bullet."

Before the D-Day invasion force sailed from Britain, the Supreme Allied Commander, American General Dwight D Eisenhower, said this to them: "… this is the year 1944! Much has happened since the Nazi triumphs of 1940 and 1941. The Allies have inflicted upon the Germans great defeats … The tide has turned! The free men of the world are marching together to victory."

Although it would be another eleven months before Germany surrendered, the Normandy landings were indeed the beginning of the end of World War II.

GLOSSARY

Allies

Countries such as Britain, France and the USA that fought together against Germany, Japan, Italy and some other countries during World War Two.

Blitzkrieg

The German army's fast advance through Europe. The word means "lightning war".

Concentration camps

Camps set up by the Nazis to kill their opponents and people they regarded as "racially impure".

Destroyer

A fast warship armed with both guns and torpedoes for sinking enemy vessels.

D-Day

Officially named "Operation Overlord". D-Day was 6 June 1944, when the Allies landed in France to begin freeing Europe from Nazi occupation.

Dictator

A leader who imposes his will on a country using military force and intimidation instead of elections.

Eastern Front

The battle ground between Nazi Germany and the USSR.

Landing craft

A flat-bottomed ship for landing troops on a beach.

Nazi

A member of Adolf Hitler's National Socialist Party and supporter of its policies.

Red Army

The army of the USSR (see below).

Resistance

People in an occupied country who secretly fight against their rulers.

USSR

The Union of Soviet Socialist Republics, often referred to as "Soviet Russia" or the "Soviet Union".

WAR AT SEA

The enemy was all around. The Luftwaffe (the German air force), the U-boats and the warships of the German navy all lay in wait. And there were always the icebergs, and the freezing fog, of the Barents Sea.

WAR ON LAND

The first wave of troops was mostly killed, cut down as they came ashore. Then the second wave of troops had to advance over the bodies of the dead. Survival was their main instinct.

WAR AT HOME

The boys had a meeting and decided to take as many knives and forks as they could get their hands on in order to defend themselves. But they realised that knives and forks would be little use against the Nazis' guns.

WAR IN THE AIR

Dundas's Spitfire began to spiral downwards, spinning wildly while he pulled and wrenched and hammered at the hood to open it. But Dundas still couldn't get the canopy open wide enough to escape through the gap.